Basic Training For walking with Jesus.

By Michel Hendricks

Contents

He is the one we proclaim, admonishing and teaching everyone with all wisdom, so that we may present everyone fully mature in Christ. To this end I strenuously contend with all the energy Christ so powerfully works in me.

Paul's letter to the church in Colossae (Colossians 1:28-29)

Introduction

Maybe a friend invited you to church or talked to you about God, and something about this person, Jesus, clicked inside you. Or maybe you started reading the Bible. Or possibly you have been walking for Jesus for years. Maybe you recently became a follower of Jesus and were baptized. Whatever your background or story may be, you now find yourself thinking, "I love who Jesus is and what he has done. I like how I feel when I talk to him and learn from him. But where do I go from here? I encountered Jesus and my life feels different, but what do I do now? How do I walk with him during the entire week? How do I grow? How do I change?" These are good questions, maybe some of the most important questions you have ever asked.

In the military, basic training is what turns civilians into soldiers. In it you are taught all of the basic skills needed to be a soldier, skills that you will use for the rest of your military career. Your life will depend on your mastery of what you learn in basic training. This is a common concept. I started playing football early in life, in second grade. I remember showing up to the first practice of a new football season. The coach, a big hulking man, had the team sit down in the middle of the field. He took his time, not speaking for several minutes, just looking us over one by one. Everyone started feeling nervous. Then he took a football, held it out in front of him, and slowly and deliberately he said, "This is a football." We all started laughing. His point was that every year we start from zero and make sure we know the basics. The first several weeks of practice were basic training on blocking, tackling, catching and throwing. Nothing more. Life is like that. Walking with Jesus is like that.

So look at the next few weeks as your basic training. These are truths and disciplines that you will return to over and over. These are the essential skills you revisit when you wander off the path. They are like guard rails keeping you from veering off the road into a ditch. They are the foundation you lay before building a house. You will use them for the rest of your life. As a follower of Jesus, you will build your life upon them. You will learn other skills in your Christian walk that are not included in this book, but you will never stop using your basic training.

And Jesus talks about that. *"Anyone who listens to my teaching and follows it is wise, like a person who builds a house on solid rock. Though the rain comes in torrents and the floodwaters rise and the winds beat against that house, it won't collapse because it is built on bedrock. But anyone who hears my teaching and doesn't obey it is foolish, like a person who builds a house on sand. When the rains and floods come and the winds beat against that house, it will collapse with a mighty crash"* (Matthew 7:24-27 NLT).

When you take the time to work through *Basic Training* and then start incorporating this teaching from Jesus into your daily life, you are building your house on a bedrock of truth that will withstand all of the suffering, garbage, betrayal, addiction, sickness and loss that life will throw at you.

You will remain standing.

How to use this book

Basic Training for Walking with Jesus is organized to be worked through a day at a time. You will see that the title of each lesson starts with "Day 1," "Day 2," etc., so each daily topic is designed to be started and completed in a single setting. For the next few weeks, I invite you to dedicate 10-15 minutes each day to allow God's word to nourish your mind and ground you in the essentials of the new life in Jesus. Each lesson contains several passages from the Bible that teach on the topic of the day. There will be several questions under each passage to encourage you to not only read the Bible but dig into it and understand it. If you don't know the answer to a question, re-read the Bible passage above the question. The answer to each question will come out of the passage above. Sometimes it will take a few readings before it sinks in. Again, the purpose of the questions is to make sure that your training in the spiritual basics is based on God's word and that you are understanding his word correctly.

At the end of each daily lesson, there is a conclusion that will wrap up the teaching. The answers to most questions will be found in the conclusion, so if you couldn't answer a question, you should find it there. You can go back to any unanswered questions and fill them in for future reference. Although *Basic Training for Walking with Jesus* is designed as a self-study, you can benefit working through this with a friend or in a small group. A possible schedule would be to work through 5 days on your own and then get together and discuss what you are learning. You can also share questions you may have or applications to your life that you want to make.

You will notice that when the Bible is quoted, several versions are used. You will see the English Standard Version (ESV), the New International Version (NIV), and the New Living Translation (NLT). These are three translations of the same original manuscripts (mostly in Hebrew and Greek), and sometimes one translation captures the essence or is easier to understand than the others. They are all good versions to read, and if you don't own a Bible, I would recommend buying one of these versions.

The fact that you are taking time out of your busy schedule to work on basic training shows that you are hungry. You desire to grow and be used by God. I am excited that you are starting this book and consider it a privilege to take you through *Basic Training for Walking With Jesus*.

So let's get started.

SECTION 1

Salvation in Jesus.

There is a threshold event in the life of every follower of Jesus. Many religions are passed down by families and are rooted in cultural tradition. You can be born that way. However, Christianity is one generation from extinction and has been since Jesus left the earth over 2000 years ago. Everyone has to work their own stuff out with Jesus. It is never passed down. It is a personal encounter between you and Jesus.

If you are starting the basic training study, we assume that you have bumped into Jesus somewhere along the path of your life. It may have happened recently as you came to church and started hearing about the truth and grace of Jesus. Or maybe it happened somewhere else, and now you have picked up this book. Whatever the case, you are here, starting this journey.

The first section of basic training focuses on this threshold event: Salvation. What is it exactly? Why do I need to be saved? Will my life change? How do I know that something happened between me and God? What if I originally felt excited and changed, but now the emotions are gone? Did I lose it? Can I lose it? We are going to look at these questions and more.

DAY 1
A new birth

Let's start like Jesus often did, with a story. It's a story about a man who was very religious. Super strict. Not like many of us. He lived in Israel during Jesus' life and heard him teach. However this man was a Jewish religious leader. A Pharisee.

As Jesus bumped into people who were messy and broken, he treated them with kindness and respect. He showed them grace and offered them a new way to live. Because of this, crowds of people were drawn to him. But there was one exception: religious leaders. Pharisees. The Pharisees were loading people with guilt and standing between them and God's love. As a result, Jesus' teachings offended them because he exposed their hypocrisy. They didn't like him.

But the religious leader in our story, unlike the other Pharisees, didn't dismiss Jesus. He was confused and intrigued by him. So let's read the story (John 3:1-4 NLT):

> There was a man named Nicodemus, a Jewish religious leader who was a Pharisee. After dark one evening, he came to speak with Jesus. "Rabbi," he said, "we all know that God has sent you to teach us. Your miraculous signs are evidence that God is with you."
>
> Jesus replied, "I tell you the truth, unless you are born again, you cannot see the Kingdom of God."

"What do you mean?" exclaimed Nicodemus. "How can an old man go back into his mother's womb and be born again?"

Notice the time of the day that Nicodemus visits Jesus. Why might this be important?

Why do you think that Nicodemus went to Jesus when most religious leaders stayed away?

How would you react to being told that you cannot see God's Kingdom unless you are born a second time?

Let's read Jesus' explanation of being born again:

Jesus replied, "Humans can reproduce only human life, but the Holy Spirit gives birth to spiritual life. So don't be surprised when I say, 'You must be born again.' The wind blows wherever it wants. Just as you can hear the wind but can't tell where it comes from or where it is going, so you can't explain how people are born of the Spirit."

"How are these things possible?" Nicodemus asked (John 3:6-9, NLT).

How might salvation be like birth?

How might wind give us a picture into spiritual birth?

Read 2 Corinthians 5:17 (NLT):

> *Anyone who belongs to Christ has become a new person. The old life is gone; a new life has begun!*

How has your life become new since belonging to Jesus?

WRAP UP

Nicodemus sneaks out at night to find Jesus, hoping that no one will see him. He doesn't want to harm his career as a Pharisee, but he's curious about Jesus. He wants to ask him questions, to understand what he is doing. But Jesus hijacks the conversation and tells him that our threshold event, our salvation and entrance into God's kingdom, is such a radical life-altering event that it can only be described as being "born again." The word "again" in the original language can mean either "again" or "from above." Most scholars think that Jesus was intentionally making a play on words. He chooses a phrase that can mean "born again" and "born from above" knowing that Nicodemus would choose the literal meaning, thinking that Jesus is saying that you have to crawl back into your mother's womb and be born a second time. But Jesus, being the genius that he is, uses the tension and confusion to make a profound point: in order to enter God's kingdom, you must experience a rebirth, a spiritual rebirth. You don't take your current belief system and add a little Jesus to it. It isn't a new hobby. Jesus isn't a spiritual guru whom you add to a long line of other spiritual gurus and religions to consult for wisdom. He offers an entirely new life requiring rebirth. When you cross the threshold and place your faith in Jesus, it is like using your spiritual eyes for the first time. It is a new life, unlike anything you have experienced before.

We find a modern analogy of this in the movie *The Matrix*. Morpheus offers Neo a chance to escape his enslaved meaningless existence. It involves a choice: take the red pill or the blue pill. But Morpheus explains that this is a choice that can alter Neo's life forever.

Morpheus: *"This is your last chance. After this, there is no turning back. You take the blue pill—the story ends, you wake up in your bed and believe whatever you want to believe. You take the red pill—you stay in Wonderland, and*

I show you how deep the rabbit hole goes. Remember, all I'm offering is the truth—nothing more."

Jesus is essentially saying the same thing. This life is not as you think it is. You have been deceived about the nature of your existence. Nicodemus couldn't grasp it. However, the Apostle Paul did grasp it: *"I am unspiritual, sold into slavery to sin"* (Romans 7:14). Only Jesus can open your eyes, free you and take you into the reality called eternal life. But it doesn't involve a little self-advancement, changing a few habits, or working on a few areas of your life. It requires a new birth, and there is no turning back.

NEXT LESSON

What is this threshold event and how can I be born from above?

DAY 2
The threshold event

The story we read yesterday doesn't end there. Jesus continues talking with Nicodemus and bluntly tells him that he doesn't understand basic concepts that a Jewish teacher should know. I'm sure that this was insulting to Nicodemus since he had a Ph.D. in religious studies, and Jesus was an uneducated carpenter. Jesus then clearly explains what this rebirth is and how it is received:

> *"For this is how God loved the world: He gave his one and only Son, so that everyone who believes in him will not perish but have eternal life. God sent his Son into the world not to judge the world, but to save the world through him. There is no judgment against anyone who believes in him. But anyone who does not believe in him has already been judged for not believing in God's one and only Son"* (John 3:16-18 NLT).

What was God's motivation for sending his Son to us?

According to John 3:16, what do we have to do to be saved and have eternal life?

Once we believe in Jesus, do we need to fear God's judgment? Why not?

Read what Jesus says in John 5:24 (NLT):

> *"I tell you the truth, those who listen to my message and believe in God who sent me have eternal life. They will never be condemned for their sins, but they have already passed from death into life."*

Now read Ephesians 2:8—9 (ESV):

> *For by grace you have been saved through faith. And this is not your own doing; it is the gift of God, not a result of works, so that no one may boast.*

Definition of *grace*: Unmerited favor. God cut us a sweet deal that we didn't work for and didn't deserve.

Definition of *faith*: Belief. Trust. Faith is living with the confidence that Jesus is who he says he is and will keep every promise that he has made to us.

What do we do to be saved?

What works do we have to do to be saved?

Why might this be hard for many of us to believe?

WRAP UP

Our salvation has love as its starting point. God was moved with love when he sent Jesus to earth, knowing that it would cost his life. It was God's plan for Jesus to carry and pay the punishment of our sins. Peter expresses it this way, *"He* (Jesus) *personally carried our sins in his body on the cross...By his wounds you are healed"* (1 Peter 2:24, NIV). Our part in receiving this healing and being born spiritually is to place our faith in what Jesus did. We simply receive the gift by faith. Faith is more than just intellectually believing the facts about Jesus' death and resurrection. It includes that but much more. Faith involves putting Jesus in the center of your life and leaning your life on him. Using another analogy, he is the only lifesaver that is able to keep you from drowning. Notice in John 3:16 Jesus describes himself as God's "one and only Son." There is no other person like Jesus. He is unique in his ability to rescue those who trust in him. God saves you through grace, meaning that he dumps blessings on you that you don't deserve and didn't earn. If you have to work to earn something, it can't be called a free gift. It is a salary. But salvation in Jesus is a gift, a free gift. When we believe in Jesus, we receive eternal life and will not be judged for our sins.

NEXT LESSON

We just studied the good news. Now the bad news...

DAY 3

The Bad News

What is wrong with us? We have studied our salvation in Jesus for the last 2 days, but why do we need to be saved in the first place? Most of us know that something is wrong with us and with the universe. Even Paul, who wrote a large part of the New Testament, describes his struggle this way, *"I don't really understand myself, for I want to do what is right, but I don't do it. Instead, I do what I hate. . . And I know that nothing good lives in me, that is, in my sinful nature. I want to do what is right, but I can't"* (Romans 7:15, 18, NLT). Why are we like this? What has happened to us?

Why do we need a savior? To a drowning person, a lifesaver makes sense. But if you look around you in our society, there are a lot of people living seemingly happy lives. They get married, have kids, go to work, and mow their lawns. Is the universe really broken? On the other hand, we see broken marriages, addiction, depression, and sickness. Is this the way life was supposed to be?

For the next few days we are going to tackle the bad news. Let's look at where all the problems started. God created the heavens and the earth. He created fish, birds and all kinds of animals. As his crowning achievement, he creates Adam and Eve. They live in perfect intimacy with God and each other in a beautiful orchard. They are naked, but they are living in a state of total harmony and acceptance, so they feel no shame. They don't even know what shame is.

This is called *shalom* – the Hebrew word for perfect peace and completeness. Adam and Eve were living in shalom.

God tells them to enjoy the fruit of thousands of types of trees. Peaches, apples, mangos, apricots, oranges, persimmons, and bananas. The only exception is the fruit from the tree in the middle of the garden, the Tree of the Knowledge of Good and Evil. Eating from this tree will kill them. Then, after some time, Satan visits them in the form of a serpent and does what he does best; he makes them forget about the thousands of trees they can eat from and focuses their attention on the one fruit they are told not eat.

> The serpent was the shrewdest of all the wild animals the Lord God had made. One day he asked the woman, "Did God really say you must not eat the fruit from any of the trees in the garden?"
>
> "Of course we may eat fruit from the trees in the garden," the woman replied. "It's only the fruit from the tree in the middle of the garden that we are not allowed to eat. God said, 'You must not eat it or even touch it; if you do, you will die.'"
>
> "You won't die!" the serpent replied to the woman. "God knows that your eyes will be opened as soon as you eat it, and you will be like God, knowing both good and evil."
>
> The woman was convinced. She saw that the tree was beautiful and its fruit looked delicious, and she

*wanted the wisdom it would give her. So she took
some of the fruit and ate it. Then she gave some to
her husband, who was with her, and he ate it, too.
At that moment their eyes were opened, and they
suddenly felt shame at their nakedness. So they
sewed fig leaves together to cover themselves*
(Genesis 3:1-7 NLT).

What is shrewd about the way the serpent reasons with Eve?

Does the serpent lie? What is the lie? What truth is contained in the lie?

Where was Adam during Eve's conversation with Satan?

Why did they suddenly feel shame for the first time in their lives? What is shame?

Where in your life is the serpent talking to you? What lies do you hear? Where is your shame?

WRAP UP

Satan slithers into paradise with a plan: to ruin it. He wants to destroy something beautiful. He wants to break the perfect shalom between the man, the woman, and their Creator. Satan is evil, but he is not stupid. He doesn't say, "Deny God and follow me, the prince of darkness. I will destroy this paradise and make you miserable." Instead he mixes truth with lies and questions the goodness of God. "Did God really say...?" means "God is holding out on you. He is keeping the good stuff for himself." It is a subtle lie. And Eve falls for it. She likes the beauty of the tree, the appearance of the fruit, and desires the wisdom of knowing good and evil. Adam abdicates his sovereignty over the orchard and stays silent. He passively watches when he should be standing between Eve and the serpent, protecting his wife.

The serpent was correct in saying that they would gain knowledge by eating the fruit. What he doesn't say is the horrible cost it would bring to the human race. The first result of their disobedience is shame. It is the pain of knowing our own failure and guilt. They suddenly realize that they are naked. They are not good enough. They have flaws. The fig leaves are humanity's first attempt at hiding ourselves, who we really are.

We have been doing this ever since.

NEXT LESSON

What is God's reaction to what just happened?

DAY 4
The bad news continued...

Let's continue reading to see how their relationship with God changes.

> *When the cool evening breezes were blowing, the man and his wife heard the Lord God walking about in the garden. So they hid from the Lord God among the trees. Then the Lord God called to the man, "Where are you?" He replied, "I heard you walking in the garden, so I hid. I was afraid because I was naked." "Who told you that you were naked?" the Lord God asked. "Have you eaten from the tree whose fruit I commanded you not to eat?" The man replied, "It was the woman you gave me who gave me the fruit, and I ate it." Then the Lord God asked the woman, "What have you done?" "The serpent deceived me," she replied. "That's why I ate it"* (Genesis 3:8-13 NLT).

What was Adam and Eve's first reaction when they heard God walking in the garden? Why?

Why do you think that God's first question after seeing what happened is, "Who told you that you were naked?"

What was Adam's excuse for his actions?

What was Eve's response to God asking her, "What have you done?"

Why do we, as humans, want to blame others for what we have done?

WRAP UP

The hiding continues. Not only do Adam and Eve hide their naked bodies from each other, they hear God taking a walk in the garden and hide themselves from him. They had never done this before, so when God calls, "Where are you?" he is expecting them to come running, excited to see him. This is likely what he has done many times in the past, but they had never hidden from him before. They had never felt naked and afraid of him. When Adam says that they hid from him because they were naked, God immediately asks them, *"Who told you that you were naked?"* God knows that there was a third party involved. No one had ever told Adam and Eve who they were except God. All of a sudden, they are accepting the label *naked* that did not come from God.

When God questions Adam further, the man blames Eve, but the way he phrases it makes it even worse. He blames "the woman you gave me," so he is passive-aggressively blaming God for his actions. Eve, in turn, blames the serpent. At least Eve stays closer to the truth, *"The serpent deceived me", she says, "That's why I ate it."* Here is where the shame/blame cycle began. Our tendency to blame someone for what we have done is a way we try to escape the consequences of our actions. We use it to try to heal our shame, but it doesn't work.

NEXT LESSON

Unfortunately, it goes from bad to worse.

DAY 5
The walking dead

The snowball of events that started with a simple act of disobedience by a man and woman in an orchard very quickly spins out of control. Once the human race disconnected itself from God, the earthly paradise was quickly lost. Shalom was broken. First came hiding and shame, then blame. Shortly thereafter, brothers killed each other. Brothers raped their sisters. Men murdered men. Men raped men. The powerful oppressed the weak. People were united in rebellion against God. Violence thundered out of control. The effects of broken shalom spread to the entire human race. This is the world in which we live.

Read Genesis 6:5-6 (NLT):

> *The Lord observed the extent of human wickedness on the earth, and he saw that everything they thought or imagined was consistently and totally evil. So the Lord was sorry he had ever made them and put them on the earth. It broke his heart.*

Why do you think that everything fell apart so quickly?

What was God's reaction to our rebellion and evil? How did he feel?

Read Romans 3:23 (NLT):

> *For everyone has sinned; we all fall short of God's glorious standard.*

What is sin according to this verse?

Who has sinned and who hasn't sinned?

Read Romans 6:23 (NLT):

> *For the wages of sin is death...*

What is the consequence of sin from this passage?

How can the Bible say that a person is dead even though they are still breathing?

Read Genesis 2:16 (NLT):

> And the LORD God commanded the man, "You are free to eat from any tree in the garden; but you must not eat from the tree of the knowledge of good and evil, for when you eat from it you will certainly die."

Why didn't Adam and Eve die when they ate the fruit?

In what way did Adam and Eve die that day?

Read Isaiah 59:2 (ESV):

> Your iniquities (sins) have made a separation
>   between you and your God,
> and your sins have hidden his face from you
>   so that he does not hear.

How have our sins altered our relational intimacy with God?

WRAP UP

God clearly tells us that we have all sinned, and the consequence of sin is death. Therefore, all have died. From a spiritual point of view, we are the walking dead. At its core, death is a separation. Physical death occurs when the soul separates from the body. Spiritual death happens when we are separated from God. The original death happened when Adam and Eve disobeyed God, and from that point on, we all enter into life as spiritually dead people. We are born dead, separated from God. After Adam and Eve sinned God led them out of paradise. They could no longer live in *shalom* with Him. The separation had started. We were never created to live separately from God, so once we started living apart from him, paradise rapidly disintegrated.

The word "sin" is an archery term used to indicate a failure to hit the bull's-eye. We miss God's perfect standard, or "we fall short of the glory of God" (Romans 3:23, ESV). The "all capitals" **SIN** is our rejection and rebellion against God, our independence from him. From this **SIN** comes many sins: greed, murder, lying, adultery, selfishness etc. But they all stem from our rejection and separation from God. Our **SIN** fleshes itself out in different sins for different people. Some of us may seem worse than others. Some people commit more obvious sins, while the sins of others are subtler or hidden. But we all start life living in a state of **SIN**.

NEXT LESSON

We will next look at God's solution to this problem.

DAY 6
God's Plan - Rescue and transfer

Was God satisfied to leave us in this broken state of shalom, separated from him? Did he give up on us? Unknown to Adam and Eve in that moment, God already had a solution. Ultimately, the plan that God hatched to recapture the human race was a rescue operation. Let's look at a few of the many ways this plan is described:

Read Colossians 1:13-14 (NLT):

> *For He has rescued us from the dominion of darkness and brought us into the kingdom of the Son He loves, in whom we have redemption, the forgiveness of sins.*

From what are we rescued in God's plan?

In what ways were we living in a *"dominion of darkness"* before we bumped into Jesus?

What are some of the results of our transfer into this new kingdom of God's Son?

Read Ephesians 2:4-5 (NIV):

> But because of His great love for us, God, who is rich in mercy, made us alive with Christ even when we were dead in transgressions (sins)–it is by grace you have been saved.

What prompted God to hatch this rescue plan?

According this scripture, what areas of our lives do we need to clean up before he will make us alive?

In what way is God's plan "rich in mercy?"

What role does grace play in our salvation?

WRAP UP

On the same day that Adam and Eve sinned, God revealed a plan to undo the serpent's damage. When God rebukes Satan for deceiving Eve, he says to the serpent, *"I will cause hostility between you and the woman, and between your offspring and her offspring. He will strike your head, and you will strike his heel"* (Genesis 3:15, NLT). This is likely a cryptic foreshadowing of God's plan, to be revealed thousands of years later. Someday a man, a son of Eve, will come who will strike the head of the serpent. He will deal a deadly blow to Satan. In the process, this man will suffer a strike on the heel. That man is Jesus! 1 John 3:8 says, *"The Son of God came to destroy the works of the devil,"* and the Son was stricken himself in the process, suffering crucifixion and death. Ultimately, death could not keep its hold on Jesus. As a result, when we place our faith in Jesus, we are transferred from the kingdom of darkness and into the kingdom of Jesus.

This entire rescue plan has love as its starting point. Since he rescued us while "we were dead" in our sins, we never even had the opportunity to earn it. A dead person cannot clean himself or herself up. It is because of this that we see the words *mercy* and *grace* often used in the Bible to describe our salvation. These two words are related but they do not mean the same thing. It is important that you understand their meanings because they are central to God's rescue plan. Mercy is shown when God doesn't give us what we deserve. He withholds punishment out of kindness and compassion. This is mercy. Grace is when God dumps blessings on us that we do not deserve and did not earn. It is unmerited favor. Our salvation is a combination of mercy and grace. Through Jesus, God removes our punishment and puts it on Jesus. He bears our punishment and our death instead of us. This is mercy. Then he grants us blessings: eternal life, forgiveness, adoption as children of God. He sends his Holy Spirit to live in us. This is grace. Once we believe in Jesus' message and are forgiven, we live in a state of grace.

Jesus' followers are people who have tasted God's mercy and grace.

NEXT LESSON

What does God do with our sin?

DAY 7
God's plan - Forgiveness

As we read yesterday in Colossians 1:13-14, one of the results of our being transferred from the kingdom of darkness into the kingdom of Jesus is our forgiveness. A broken relationship requires forgiveness in order for it to be repaired in a healthy way. We have already studied that we have all sinned and that the result of our sin is separation from God. The path to repair this broken shalom is through forgiveness. Jesus provides a plan through which God forgives all of our sins – past, present, and future. This is what we will study today.

Read the following verses:

> In him (Jesus) we have redemption through his blood, the forgiveness of sins, in accordance with the riches of God's grace that he lavished on us (Ephesians 1:7 NIV).

> All the prophets testify about him (Jesus) that everyone who believes in him receives forgiveness of sins through his name (Acts 10:43).

What is forgiveness?

Why is forgiveness an act of grace? (See the definition of grace from yesterday)

What do we need to do in order to be forgiven by God?

Read Colossians 2:13-14 (NLT):

> *You were dead because of your sins . . . Then God made you alive with Christ, for he forgave all our sins. He canceled the record of the charges against us and took it away by nailing it to the cross.*

Which of our sins are forgiven when we trust in Jesus? Which are not? What about future sins?

What is this "record of charges against us" in Colossians 2:13-14?

Why would our record be nailed to the cross? What does this signify?

Read Isaiah 1:18 (ESV):

> Though your sins are like scarlet,
> I will make them as white as snow.

What is the meaning of God changing the color of our sins?

WRAP-UP

The word *forgive* is defined: "letting sins go as if they had never been committed. Taking away the penalty." When we forgive someone, we relinquish our claim for revenge. We no longer bring it up in order to make the person feel bad because the matter is done and settled. When God forgives us, he will no longer hold a claim against us or bring it up. This results in a restoration of trust and intimacy. So what happens to our sins? Paul describes it in shocking language in Colossians 2:13-14 that you studied above: *"He canceled the record of the charges against us and took it away by nailing it to the cross."* The "record of charges" is also translated "certificate of debt." It is the record of all of our offenses. It is the sum total of every sinful, selfish act that we have committed. God takes this record, which for most of us is a large volume, and he nails it to the cross. The effect couldn't be more graphic. The cross was used for executions, like our modern day electric chair. The cross was used to kill Jesus, and in that act, God poured all of our sins onto him. When we trust and receive Jesus, our record of charges is metaphorically nailed to the cross and dies with Jesus. The last thing Jesus said before he died on the cross was *"tetelestai"* which means "It is finished." This is Jesus' declaration of "Paid in Full" stamped on our record of charges. Our debt has been paid and we are now free from that burden.

Your reaction might be, "OK. I see that my sins are forgiven when I come to Jesus, but what about my future sins? Didn't he just pay my past sins? What if I screw up in the future?" That is a good question and one that pastors hear often. First of all, think about when Jesus paid for our sins. It happened over 2000 years ago, so at that time *all* of our sins were future sins. Second, Jesus didn't just deal with our specific sins. He also dealt with our sin issue, our **SIN**. So when we sin after coming to Jesus, it is no longer treated as a moral debt that needs to be nailed to the cross. It has already been paid in full. Our scarlet sins have been made white. When we sin after our salvation, we handle it in a completely different way. We will study how we handle our sin as a saved follower of Jesus in a future lesson.

NEXT LESSON

More on our salvation.

DAY 8
God's plan - Ransom and Peace

Our salvation is so immense, so overwhelmingly beautiful and surprising that the Bible uses many different metaphors to describe it. It cannot be described in a few sentences. We have already seen that our salvation is a rescue plan with the aim of transferring us from the kingdom of darkness into the kingdom of Jesus. It brings us forgiveness for everything wrong we have ever done and will do. Today we will look at two more aspects of our salvation: Ransom and restored peace.

Read Mark 10:45 (NIV) (Jesus is speaking):

> *For even the Son of Man (Jesus) did not come to be served but to serve, and to give his life as a ransom for many.*

Read 1 Timothy 2:5-6 (NIV):

> *For there is one God and one mediator between God and mankind, the man Christ Jesus, who gave himself as a ransom for all people.*

From Mark 10:45 what was Jesus' primary purpose for coming to earth?

If we needed a ransom to be paid, what does that say about us?

What was our ransom? What was the price for our release?

What does the price say about our value to God?

Read Romans 5:1-2, 10 (NLT):

> *Therefore, since we have been made right in God's sight by faith, we have peace with God because of what Jesus Christ our Lord has done for us. Because of our faith, Christ has brought us into this place of undeserved privilege where we now stand, and we confidently and joyfully look forward to sharing God's glory. . . For since our friendship with God was restored by the death of his Son while we were still his enemies, we will certainly be saved through the life of his Son.*

In what ways were we like God's enemies before being rescued?

In your experience, how do two enemies become friends?

Who initiated the peace between us and God?

What did we do to bring about this peace?

WRAP UP

Before our rescue, we were living as hostages. When you are a hostage, you don't live where you belong. In movies, hostages typically end up in a dank basement with duct tape wrapped around their mouths. As a hostage you don't have power over your life. You do not have freedom until the ransom is paid. This is true for us in the spiritual realm of our lives. Our spirit is not in the right place, and we are in bondage. Jesus makes it clear that his primary purpose for coming to earth was to pay our ransom in order to set us free. He did this by dying on the cross and rising from the dead. In spiritual currency, this paid our ransom and set us free. The fact that God allowed his son to give his life for us shows how valuable we are to him.

This ransom not only frees us, it also brings peace between us and God. Before being set free we were living as enemies of God. But he does not give up on us. Instead, he converts his enemies into his children whom he loves. Usually in our world, it takes effort from both sides for enemies to become friends. However, God makes peace with us with no effort or cooperation on our part. He initiates peace with us while we are still his enemies. We are spiritually dead, and he approaches us and raises us up from the dead. We aren't saved because we earned it. We aren't saved by cooperating with God. God doesn't go halfway and wait for us to meet him halfway. We are saved because he saves us. He goes all the way, and we are rescued. A hostage can't meet a rescuer halfway. Spiritually speaking, we are tied up with duct tape over our mouths. We aren't going anywhere unless someone rescues us. As we studied before, God saves us by grace. He dumps blessings on us that we do not deserve. How great is God's grace!

NEXT LESSON

Can I lose it?

DAY 9

Can I lose the greatest gift?

So you believe that you've received this awesome gift of life through Jesus. He has forgiven all of your sins (past, present, and future), and has given you eternal life. Your ransom has been paid by Jesus, and you now have peace with God. You have been adopted as his child. So here are questions I often hear: Can I lose this gift? What if I do something wrong? What if I lie? What if I cheat on a test? Or look at porn? Or have an affair? Can it be taken away if I murder someone? If I'm addicted to something, shouldn't my salvation heal my addiction? If not, does it mean I'm not really saved?

These are great questions and are useful to sharpen our understanding of our salvation and our relationship with God. This is what we will study today.

Read John 6:39-40 (NLT) (Jesus speaking):

> *And this is the will of God, that I should not lose even one of all those he has given me, but that I should raise them up at the last day. For it is my Father's will that all who see his Son and believe in him should have eternal life. I will raise them up at the last day.*

What is God's will for Jesus in John 6:39-40?

What is the chance that Jesus will fail in this and lose someone that the Father has given him?

Jesus calls people who follow him *"my sheep."*

> *My sheep listen to my voice; I know them, and they follow me. I give them eternal life, and they will never perish. No one can snatch them away from me, for my Father has given them to me, and he is more powerful than anyone else. No one can snatch them from the Father's hand. The Father and I are one* (John 10:27-30, NLT).

What could cause Jesus' sheep to perish?

Who is able to snatch us out of Jesus hand?

Since we are also in the Father's hand, who is able to snatch us out of the Father's hand?

Is being in Jesus' hand a safe position?

Read 1 John 5:11-13:

> And this is the testimony: God has given us eternal life, and this life is in his Son. Whoever has the Son has life; whoever does not have the Son of God does not have life. I write these things to you who believe in the name of the Son of God so that you may know that you have eternal life.

Who has eternal life according to 1 John 5:11-13?

What is the difference between *hoping* that we have eternal life, versus *knowing* we have eternal life?

Why might God want us to *know* it instead of just hoping for it?

WRAP UP

Once we come to Jesus and place our faith in him, our position is secure. It is something we can know, not just hope. Jesus himself is charged by God with the task of not losing a single person whom God has given him. The picture Jesus paints in John 10 is vivid. We are in Jesus' hand, and no one can snatch us out. In addition to this, we are in the Father's hand, which we can envision being wrapped around Jesus' hand which is wrapped around us. So to separate us from Jesus, someone would have to break God's grip and then break Jesus' grip. There is no one in the universe, including ourselves, with the power to break both Jesus' and God's hold on us. Can you think of a more secure position? The apostle Paul asks, *"Who can separate us from the love of Christ?"* He answers in Romans 8:38-39 (NLT):

> *I am convinced that nothing can ever separate us from God's love. Neither death nor life, neither angels nor demons, neither our fears for today nor our worries about tomorrow—not even the powers of hell can separate us from God's love. No power in the sky above or in the earth below—indeed, nothing in all creation will ever be able to separate us from the love of God that is revealed in Christ Jesus our Lord.*

So can you lose your salvation once Jesus has rescued you, adopted you, and made you a new creation? Can you be un-forgiven, un-adopted as God's child, and un-rescued? The answer is NO. What if you mess up in a big way? Scott Nickell, a pastor friend of mine, sums it up this way: "*You didn't gain your salvation by your good performance. You can't lose it by your bad performance.*" However, there are consequences for our behavior. You might end up in jail or lose your marriage. That is exactly why God gives us guard rails in life that we are to stay between to keep us from wrecking ourselves. But our salvation is untouchable and secure. There is no one in the entire universe with the power to separate us from God. This is good news indeed!

> "*You didn't gain your salvation by your good performance. You can't lose it by your bad performance.*"
>
> Scott Nickell

NEXT LESSON

We have been studying salvation. Now let's take several weeks to look at the one who came up with this idea.

SECTION 2

God 101

We have been studying our salvation that God provided through his son Jesus. Now let's take a few days and focus on the one who planned this whole rescue mission. Who is God? What is he like? Has anyone ever seen him? Is Jesus God or just a really good person? If Jesus is God, how can he also be God's Son? How does that make sense? Who is the Holy Spirit?

You will notice Bible verses in parentheses like this (John 3:16). When learning about God, Jesus, and the Holy Spirit, it is important to realize that our knowledge of God is based on what the Bible teaches. You can look up every passage that is included as you are reading, or you can look them up later for your future study.

DAY 10
Who is God?

That is the ultimate question isn't it? Who is God? What is he like? Does he like us or is he mad at us? Is he involved in our lives or did he just wind things up and let them run? We don't know everything about God and never will, but we do know some things. He has revealed many aspects of who he is to us, and we are going to look at some of those today.

Read Genesis 1:1 (NLT):

> In the beginning God created the heavens and the earth.

Read Nehemiah 9:6 (NLT):

> You alone are the Lord. You made the skies and the heavens and all the stars. You made the earth and the seas and everything in them. You preserve them all, and the angels of heaven worship you.

What do we learn about God from the fact that he created everything?

Is there anything that he did not make?

In your opinion why did he create the universe?

Read Psalm 103:8, 11, 12:

> The LORD is compassionate and merciful,
>   slow to get angry and filled with unfailing love.

> For his unfailing love toward those who fear him
>   is as great as the height of the heavens above
> the earth.

> The Lord is like a father to his children,
>   tender and compassionate to those who fear
> him.

Do the descriptions of God in Psalm 103 conform to how you picture God?

Do you ever envision God as angry at you or impatient? If so, why?

Think of a love that is as high as the *"heavens above the earth"* What does it look and feel like?

Do you think of God as a compassionate and tender father? Why or why not?

Read 1 John 4:9-10:

> *God showed how much he loved us by sending his one and only Son into the world so that we might have eternal life through him. This is real love—not that we loved God, but that he loved us and sent his Son as a sacrifice to take away our sins.*

What motivated God to send his son to die for us?

God allowed his son to be sacrificed for us. What does this reveal about his love for us?

WRAP UP

Who is God? What is he like? Depending on your background and childhood, you may see God in a certain way. To some people he is an angry and impatient judge, just waiting for us to mess up. To others he is distant and indifferent. He isn't really involved in our lives on a daily basis.

There are many aspects of God's character, but there is one that precedes all others: love. At his core, God is a loving, compassionate, tender father. He initiates with us and is involved in the intimate details of our lives. Many people who come through the doors of a church and have a hard time believing this. How can God not be angry with me? An important goal in *Basic Training* is that you see God correctly. What is your first reaction when someone asks you what God is like? If "love" isn't in the first sentence that comes out of your mouth, then welcome to *Basic Training*. It is time to line up your thinking with what the Bible teaches.

This love is revealed in the creation. Think about it. Why did God create the universe? Was he lonely or bored? What was his primary motivation? God rejoiced as he created the world. He wasn't sad or lonely. He kept remarking about how good everything was. Then, as his crowning achievement, he creates Adam and Eve and tells them to enjoy all that he has made. God's primary motivation for creating our world is to share his love and goodness with us.

His love is so great that he does not want to keep it for himself. He wants us to see and enjoy his beauty and love.

Why did God send his son, Jesus? Just like with the creation, his motivation was love. 1 John 4:9-10 that you read above makes this clear. Romans 5:8 (NLT) says it this way: *"But God showed his great love for us by sending Christ to die for us while we were still sinners."* So God's decision to send Jesus to the world is the ultimate expression of his love for people who don't deserve his love. Think about that the next time you feel that God is angry with you. If God sacrificed his son for you while you were still a sinner and had no opportunity to clean your life up, why be stuck with the image that God is angry with you? It is true that God is emotionally complex, and those emotions include happiness, sadness, anger, and jealousy. But God leads with love and grace. That is what we see from Jesus, and it is the first sentence of the good news: God isn't angry with you. He loves you. Our story with God doesn't start with, "You are a sinner." It starts with "God loves you and invites you to come to him, sit down, and talk with him over dinner." Jesus says it this way, "Here I am! I stand at the door and knock. If anyone hears my voice and opens the door, I will come in and eat with that person, and they with me" (Revelation 3:20).

This is good news!

NEXT LESSON

What more can I know about God?

DAY 11
God 102

When answering the question, "Who is God and what is he like?" we concluded that his love is the starting point. It is the overwhelming and primary characteristic of our creator and Father. It is the first thing he wants us to know about him. However, the study doesn't end there. He has revealed more than just his love to us. Today we will look at other aspects of himself that God has revealed to us. Obviously we will not exhaust this topic. I want to whet your appetite for future study and growth. You will find, as you walk with him, that he will continue teaching you about himself for the rest of your life. But you have to start somewhere.

Read Isaiah 40:28 (NLT):

> *The Lord is the everlasting God,*
> *the Creator of all the earth.*
> *He never grows weak or weary.*
> *No one can measure the depths of his*
> *understanding.*

How old is God? What does it mean to be "everlasting" or "eternal?"

What limits are there on his strength or understanding? Why is this important?

Read Malachi 3:6 (NLT):

> I am the LORD, and I do not change.

Why would God want us to know that he does not change?

Isn't change a good thing?

Read Jeremiah 23:24 (NLT):

> Can anyone hide from me in a secret place?
> Am I not everywhere in all the heavens and
> earth?" says the Lord.

Why do we need to know that God is everywhere at once? What difference does this make?

Read Deuteronomy 32:4 (NLT):

> He is the Rock; his deeds are perfect.
>   Everything he does is just and fair.
> He is a faithful God who does no wrong;
>   how just and upright he is!

What does it mean that God is just?

Read John 1:18 (NIV):

> No one has ever seen God, but the one and only Son, who is himself God and is in closest relationship with the Father, has made him known.

Has anyone ever seen God? Why is this important?

How can you have a relationship with someone you have never seen?

WRAP UP

The concept of someone being "everlasting" or "eternal" is foreign to us. We have never met anyone who was eternal, and even our universe, once thought to be eternal, is now believed to have a beginning. Eternal means having no beginning and no end. God is eternal in both directions. He has existed forever in the past and will exist forever in the future. We can't wrap our minds around this, but nonetheless it is true.

Not only is God eternal (not limited by time), his power and understanding have no limits as well. Here on earth, we live with limits. We have to rest and eat to gain strength. God never loses strength or wears out. His understanding has no bounds. He is also everywhere at once, so his personal location has no limits. God is never so busy attending to another person that he has no time for you. He doesn't have this human limitation. All of these powers are used under the orchestration of his love and support of us. This is explained well in 2 Chronicles 16:9 (NIV), *"For the eyes of the Lord range throughout the earth to strengthen those whose hearts are fully committed to him."*

When God says that he does not change, this is meant to contrast him from us. He is utterly dependable. Unlike us, he is perfect and needs no improvement. For us, change is often good if it includes growth and maturity. Change is not always a bad thing. But with God, there is no need to change. In this aspect he is different from us.

His perfection includes his moral standing and judgments. He is completely fair and just. There is no corruption or unfaithfulness with him. He doesn't play games with us or deceive us. Notice that all of these characteristics come at the service of his love for us.

It is interesting that God is invisible to us, but Jesus came to make him known. We can make no image or painting that does justice to God's form. God is spirit (John 4:24), so he doesn't inhabit a physical body like we do. This does not limit our ability to know him, since he has been revealed to us by Jesus.

We could continue studying God and his character for many days, however I think that you get the point. As you walk with Jesus over time, you will increase in your knowledge of God. And this is God's desire for you (Colossians 1:10, 2 Peter 3:18).

NEXT LESSON

Where does Jesus fit in?

DAY 12
Jesus – A unique person

After studying the nature of our salvation, we are going to take a deeper look at the person who is the central figure of our salvation: Jesus. So who exactly is he and what makes him special? Is he God or is he man? Can he be both? What is his relationship with God his Father? Why did Jesus have such power? Today we will look into this man.

Read John 1:1-2, 14 (NIV):

> *In the beginning was the Word, and the Word was with God, and the Word was God. He was with God in the beginning . . . The Word became flesh and made his dwelling among us.*

Jesus is called "the Word" in this passage. What does this say about him?

How can the Word be with God and be God at the same time?

Read John 1:18 (NIV):

> *No one has ever seen God, but the one and only*
> *Son, who is himself God and is in closest*
> *relationship with the Father, has made him known.*

What can you learn about Jesus' relationship to his Father from this passage?

What is unique about Jesus compared to all other people?

Read Colossians 1:15 (NIV):

> *The Son is the image of the invisible God, the*
> *firstborn over all creation. For in him all things*
> *were created . . . all things have been created*
> *through him and for him. He is before all things,*
> *and in him all things hold together.*

Read John 1:3 (NIV):

> *Through him (Jesus) all things were made; without*
> *him nothing was made that has been made.*

What does it mean that Jesus is *"the image of the invisible God?"*

What is Jesus' role in the creation of the universe?

What does it mean that Jesus is *"before all things?"*

Who created Jesus? Was Jesus created?

WRAP UP

We studied that God is a loving compassionate Father. Jesus, on the other hand, is called "the Son." Jesus' relationship to God is described as a Father-Son relationship. The Father rejoices over his Son and is well pleased in him (Matthew 3:17). Jesus wants to glorify God and complete all of his work (John 17:4). The Father and the Son knew each other before the creation of the earth (John 17:5). So, unlike us, Jesus had a conscious existence before he was born. His life did not start with his birth. He enjoyed an intimate relationship with his Father before he was on earth.

As you read above, Jesus is clearly called God in John 1:1. He has attributes that are only used of God. For example he created the universe. There is nothing that has been created that he did not create. Jesus is mentioned as being in the beginning with God. He wasn't part of creation. He is eternal just like his Father. He receives worship (Matthew 28:16-17), which only God can receive (Matthew 4:10). He forgives sins (Mark 2:5-7), which only God can do. He was called God by his disciples (John 20:28), and he doesn't correct them for this. He is called God by the writers of the New Testament (Titus 2:11-14). The only conclusion we can make is that he is God. He is divine. So it is as simple as that. Or is it?

There are other aspects of Jesus that, on the surface, don't seem true of God. He gets tired and thirsty (John 4:6-7). He gets hungry (Matthew 4:2). He can only be in one place at a time. There are some things that he doesn't know (Matthew 24:36). Hmm. This doesn't sound like God. Didn't we just study that God never gets tired? Isn't God everywhere at once? Doesn't God know everything? So what is the answer? Is Jesus God or is he a man? The answer is both. Jesus is fully God and fully man. He is God in human flesh. He is fully God (Colossians 2:9) and fully human (1 John 1:1), a union of two natures in one integrated person. Jesus shows frailties that God doesn't have because, in order to become fully human, he chooses to not take advantage of some of his divine powers. He limits himself to become human. It is explained in Philippians 2:5-8 (NIV), *"In your relationships with one another, have the same mindset as Christ Jesus: Who, being in very nature God, did not consider equality with God something to be used to his own advantage; rather, he made himself nothing by taking the very nature of a servant, being made in human likeness. And being found in appearance as a man, he humbled himself by becoming obedient to death— even death on a cross!"* Because of this, he displays the perfect image of God for the world to see and understand. That is why we can know a God whom we have never seen. When someone asks you "What is God like?" the answer to give is, "Look at Jesus. Look at what he did and what he said. He is the perfect representation of God."

Some of this might not make sense, and you probably have questions. How can Jesus be God and the Son of God at the same time? How can God have a relationship with God? Are there two Gods? If there is one God, how is this explained? What if I can't understand it?

NEXT LESSON

Before we answer these questions, let's get an even broader picture.

DAY 13
The Holy spirit

If God appeared to you and gave you a choice, which would you prefer: Jesus physically with you or God living inside you? It sounds pretty appealing to have Jesus come back to earth and be with you to help you, to answer your questions, to bring his power to heal you and everyone around you. You can't be blamed for choosing Jesus. Interestingly Jesus himself answered this question for us.

Read John 14:15-17, 26 (NIV) (Jesus speaking):

> *If you love me, keep my commands. And I will ask the Father, and he will give you another advocate to help you and be with you forever – the Spirit of truth. The world cannot accept him, because it neither sees him nor knows him. But you know him, for he lives with you and will be in you . . . But the Advocate, the Holy Spirit, whom the Father will send in my name, will teach you all things and will remind you of everything I have said to you.*

Read John 16:7 (ESV) (Jesus speaking):

> *Nevertheless, I tell you the truth: it is to your advantage that I go away, for if I do not go away, the Helper will not come to you. But if I go, I will send him to you. And when he comes, he will*

convict the world concerning sin and righteousness and judgment.

What is the Holy Spirit going to do for us?

Where does the Spirit come from?

Will the Spirit ever leave us? Is there any reason he might leave us?

Is the Holy Spirit an impersonal force, like The Force in Star Wars? If not, what is he/it?

Why might it be better for Jesus to leave earth and the Holy Spirit to be sent to us?

What does it look like for the Holy Spirit to convict us of sin?

Read what Jesus says to his disciples in Acts 1:8 (NLT) shortly before he leaves earth:

> But you will receive power when the Holy Spirit comes upon you. And you will be my witnesses, telling people about me everywhere—in Jerusalem, throughout Judea, in Samaria, and to the ends of the earth.

What do we receive from the Holy Spirit?

When we receive power from the Holy Spirit, what is that power used for?

WRAP UP

The first thing you need to realize from the passages above is that the Holy Spirit is referred to as "him" not "it." He is a person not an impersonal force. He has emotions (Ephesians 4:30) and a will (Acts 16:6). He comes from the Father to live in us. After Jesus rose from the dead and ascended to the Father, he sent the Holy Spirit to his followers. So when you believed in Jesus and were saved, one of the things that happened is that God sent his Holy Spirit to live in you. He isn't just *with* you; he is *in* you. That is why you often feel "different" after coming to Jesus. God's Spirit, who didn't live in you before, came and took up residence in your life. It is a brand-new thing in your life. It is like a new birth. In fact, it is a new birth.

After his resurrection, Jesus says that it is better for him to leave earth and send the Holy Spirit to live in us. One reason this is better is that if the Spirit is living in each follower of Jesus, each of us has God's power available to us. Unlike Jesus, the Spirit has no physical body and can be everywhere at once. So his power is currently working in my life as I type this lesson (in an airplane coming home from Mexico), and at the same time he is empowering a Chinese Christian in Beijing to be a witness for Jesus there. He is helping a young woman in Argentina believe that she is not defined by the words of her ex-boyfriend, and he is helping a man in India turn off his computer and reconnect with his wife and child. The Holy Spirit empowers us to be Jesus all over the world. That is exactly what is happening in our world as you read this lesson. The Holy Spirit is given to us "forever," which means that he will never leave us. You will never be without your Helper, no matter how dark life gets.

Notice also that the Spirit is called our Helper. That is his purpose, and he helps us in many ways. We read above that he gives us power to be witnesses for Jesus, being ambassadors for Jesus' kingdom here on earth. An important task God gives us is to spread the good news about Jesus' love and grace to a lost and broken world. The Holy Spirit gives us power to do that. We are not on our own to accomplish that task. The Spirit also helps us by convicting us of our sin. After you came to Jesus, did you start noticing that there were many things in your life that needed to change? This is the Holy Spirit at work in you. Being freed from sin that entangles us results in a better life. It may be painful to break free from bad habits, but the end result is worth the pain. He convicts us of sins so that we can confess them and start leaving them behind. He gives us power to change. The Holy Spirit also prays for us (Romans 8:27), helps us apply scripture to our lives (1 Corinthians 2:14-15), and gives us power to experience joy in suffering (1 Thessalonians 1:6).

The Bible also clearly teaches that the Holy Spirit is God. He is referred to as God in the Bible (Acts 5:3-4; 1 Corinthians 2:4-5, 3:16-17) and is mentioned equally with the Father and the Son (Matthew 28:19).

NEXT LESSON

Now that this has totally confused you, let's look at the relationship between the Father, the Son, and the Holy Spirit and see what God's word says about this.

DAY 14

Where is the connection?
(God/Jesus/Holy Spirit)

So now we get to the confusing part. The Bible very clearly addresses God the Father, Jesus, and the Holy Spirit as God. Each one individually is called God. They each have qualities that are only true of God. Yet they are all different in some ways. How can three persons be called God? Are there three Gods? I thought that God said over and over in the Old Testament that he is one. There is no other God than he. Which is it? Is he one or three? Can there be one God in three persons, and if so, what does it show us about God? This is what we will look into today.

Read Isaiah 43:10 (NIV):

> *Before me no god was formed, nor will there be one after me.*

Read Deuteronomy 6:4 (NIV):

> *Hear, O Israel: The LORD our God, the LORD is one.*

How many Gods are there?

Will any other Gods ever exist besides the one God?

Read Matthew 28:19 (NIV):

> Therefore go and make disciples of all nations, baptizing them in the name of the Father and of the Son and of the Holy Spirit.

What is significant about the names in which we baptize someone?

Why not just baptize someone in the name of God?

Read 2 Corinthians 13:14 (NIV):

> May the grace of the Lord Jesus Christ, and the love of God, and the fellowship of the Holy Spirit be with you all.

How do God the Father, Jesus, and the Holy Spirit work together to bless us?

WRAP UP

So now we get to some complicated stuff. No one ever said that our God was simplistic and easy to grasp. Our one God, the Creator of the universe, consists of three co-equal persons – Father, Son, and Holy Spirit. They are equally divine, as we have studied in the previous lessons, and they live in intimate union with one another. The Father sent his Son to earth to restore broken *shalom* between humans and God. Jesus asks the Father to send the Holy Spirit to his followers to be a helper. Jesus' purpose on earth is to glorify God and accomplish all of the work the Father has given him. The Holy Spirit helps us grow in our knowledge of God and relate to our heavenly Father as our daddy (Galatians 4:6).

Are you starting to get the picture? Each is a person, relating individually to us, and fulfilling distinct but harmonious functions. So even God, before he created us or anything else, lived in deep intimacy and relational connectedness within himself. As part of his essence God is relational. For this reason, when he created the universe, he didn't do it because he was lonely or bored. He was completely content and full of joy. He created our universe to share this perfect shalom with us.

This is hard for us to grasp because we need others to enjoy relational intimacy, and we, in our being, are one person only. But God is one God in three persons. They are not three manifestations of God or aspects of God's character. They are three persons who are fully God.

There are a few helpful but imperfect analogies we can use to explain this three-in-one concept, called the trinity. One is the concept of H_2O, which exists as water, ice, and vapor. All three are H_2O, but they are different from each other. Water is not vapor, and vapor is not ice. But they are all H_2O. Obviously, this analogy is imperfect. God is a person, not an impersonal element. The three persons of the Godhead are in relationship with each other, not simply three forms of the same substance.

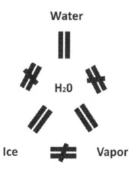

Another analogy is we human beings. We exist as a body, soul, and spirit. My body, soul and spirit are all me. The limit of this analogy is that my body, soul, and spirit are not three persons, and someday my body will die, and I will receive a new imperishable body.

So you get the point that it is complex and hard to understand, but there are some analogies in nature that can illumine aspects of the trinity. There is mystery in this doctrine, and you will have to learn to live with that. Luckily, you do not need to grasp everything about God in order to enjoy his love and grace.

NEXT LESSON

How do I grow as a follower of Jesus?

SECTION 3

Now what? (How we mature)

So you have come to Jesus, and you've believed in him and his message. As a result, you have been saved, forgiven, and granted eternal life. So what's next? Do we just wait around until we die so that we can be with Jesus in heaven? For Jesus, eternal life is never something we have to die in order to enjoy. It begins the day you start following him and are saved. As a matter of fact, most of his teachings address how important it is to spend our time and strength learning to live in his kingdom here on earth. He wants us to grow in our knowledge of him. Jesus' goal for us is well describe by Paul, who was a church planter in the first century. In his letter to the church in the city of Colossae, he writes this:

> *He (Jesus) is the one we proclaim, admonishing and teaching everyone with all wisdom, so that we may present everyone fully mature in Christ. To this end I strenuously contend with all the energy Christ so powerfully works in me.*

> Colossians 1:28-29

The goal that God has for every person who is saved by Jesus is this word, mature. Jesus wants his church to be full of people who are growing to maturity. We may not be there yet, but we are on the path. God will help us along this path to maturity, but he will not do it for us. This is work that God has given us to do. You might ask, "How do

I mature as a follower of Jesus?" This is a good question, and it is one that you will be answering for the rest of your life. In this last section of *Basic Training*, you will learn the first steps toward becoming mature in Christ. These are just first steps. There are many more practices and habits you will incorporate into your life that are not included in this book. The community of believers you have around you will help you in this path beyond the first steps.

God wants us to use the gifts he has given us to do the work of his kingdom on earth. He wants us to learn to love others like he loved people. He even wants us to learn how to love our enemies. Our relationship with him is never static. We are meant to grow, from the day we bump into Jesus for the first time until our last breath. In this section we will look at the basics of how we grow to maturity.

DAY 15
Oh no, I did it again. (Confession)

We have found that our salvation is secure. Once we bump into Jesus and believe in him, we are held safely in the encircled hands of God and Jesus. So we know that we cannot be snatched away from him, even when we mess up. We also know that ALL of our sins are forgiven (past, present, and future). But what about those future sins? We know that they are forgiven and cleansed, but how do we handle them? What do I do if I sin? Is God mad at me? Maybe I'm convinced that I haven't lost my salvation, but why do I continue to mess up? What does God want me to do when I sin? When we don't handle our sin properly we get stuck in our growth. In the next few lessons of *Basic Training*, we will show you what God wants us to do when we screw up.

Read what John, one of Jesus' closest friends, writes to a church in 1 John 1:8-2:1 (NLT):

> *If we claim we have no sin, we are only fooling*
> *ourselves and not living in the truth. But if we*
> *confess our sins to him, he is faithful and just to*
> *forgive us our sins and to cleanse us from all*
> *wickedness. If we claim we have not sinned, we are*
> *calling God a liar and showing that his word has no*
> *place in our hearts. My dear children, I am writing*
> *this to you so that you will not sin. But if anyone*
> *does sin, we have an advocate who pleads our case*

before the Father. He is Jesus Christ, the one who is
truly righteous.

What is wrong with a person who says they have no sin in their life?

What are we supposed to do when we sin?

What is confession? How do we do it and why?

What does God do if we confess our sin?

Read an example of confession by King David in Psalm 51. David was a king of Israel who committed adultery and killed a man trying to cover it up. This is his prayer of confession to God:

> *Have mercy on me, O God, because of your*
> *unfailing love. Because of your great*

compassion, blot out the stain of my sins.
Wash me clean from my guilt. Purify me from my
sin. For I recognize my rebellion; it haunts me day
and night. Against you, and you alone, have I
sinned; I have done what is evil in your sight. . .
Purify me from my sins, and I will be clean; wash
me, and I will be whiter than snow. Oh, give me
back my joy again; you have broken me— now let
me rejoice. Don't keep looking at my sins. Remove
the stain of my guilt. Create in me a clean heart, O
God. Renew a loyal spirit within me.

What do you see in David's heart as he confesses?

What excuses does David make for his sin?

What can you learn from David's example of confession?

WRAP UP

When we first come to Jesus, we come carrying the full burden of our sins. Through Jesus, this burden is removed and nailed to the cross. Our sins are paid in full, and we are free from that burden. That is good news! Unfortunately, we don't instantly become perfect sinless people after that. However, when we sin after our salvation, we handle it in a completely different way. Instead of running away from God, we run to him. We confess our sin. In Greek, the original language of the New Testament, the word *confess* is *homologeo*. It is a combination of two words. *Homo* means *"same,"* and *logeo* is the verb *"to say."* So *homologeo* means *"to say the same."* When we confess we simply are saying the same thing that God says about our sin. Confessing just means that we agree with God about our sin – we don't try to hide it from God or blame someone else or make excuses. We don't blame our childhood or our circumstances. We own it, just like David did. There are no excuses in his confession. 1 John 1:8-2:1 teaches that we should try not to sin, but if we do sin, we have an advocate who will defend us: Jesus. Even when we sin, Jesus is on our side, defending us.

Notice that the Bible never teaches that we need to go to church to confess, or that we need to sit down in a small wooden booth, slide a window, and tell a priest our sins. As far as we know, David's confession was between him and God. No one else was present. Confession involves talking openly with God about your sin. We see that David agrees with God about his sin. He is being completely honest and transparent about his failure. When we confess we agree about two things concerning our sin: 1) It is sin. 2) It is forgiven.

Check out the Frequently Asked Questions about confession on the following page.

FAQ - FREQUENTLY ASKED QUESTIONS ON CONFESSION

If we are already forgiven, why should we confess?

To restore relational intimacy with God, who is our Father. Confession maintains a healthy growing relationship with God, who has already forgiven us.

Are we forgiven because we confess? I thought that we were already forgiven.

Yes and no. We are already forgiven when we believe in Jesus. The penalty for our sins is paid in full once and for all when we come to Jesus. However, there is another sense of forgiveness. When my son does something wrong to me, I don't reject him as my son and disown him. He will always be my son. However, I want him to own what he did in order to restore our relational intimacy. I want him to tell me what he did wrong because it repairs our friendship and helps him grow. So as followers of Jesus, when we sin, we confess to come clean to God and restore our intimacy. That is the purpose of confession. We will always be his children once we believe in Jesus and are adopted as children of God. That will never change. But we confess when we realize that we have sinned in order to maintain our relational intimacy with God.

How often should we confess? Once a month? Every hour?

We confess when we realize that we have sinned. This will happen regularly, maybe daily. Sometimes the Holy Spirit will convict you of something. When you read the Bible, often you will become aware of an area of your life that doesn't line up with God's teaching. Other times a friend will say something to you. Or sometimes you may feel that something is "off" between you and God, and you will ask him to show you if you have done something wrong. He will show you. The bottom line is that we confess as soon as we are aware of a sin. You can do it as you are driving, taking a shower, or shoveling snow. You don't need to go to church. However, once you confess it, the issue has been taken care of forever. Don't confess it again. God accepts your confession.

What if I confess but I still feel guilty?

God gives us his word that if we confess our sins, he will forgive us and cleanse us (1 John 1:9). This is a fact, just like 2 + 2 = 4. You cannot change it. So if you still feel guilty about something you have already confessed, this might be pointing to an area of growth and study for you: Why can't I accept forgiveness? Or maybe: Why do I always feel guilty? These are common struggles for us, but God offers great strength to overcome these thought patterns. Also, be honest with God about your feelings. Tell him that you don't feel forgiven even though you know you are forgiven.

What if I die in a car wreck, and I have sins that I haven't confessed?

If you have placed your faith in Jesus, your sins are forgiven. Period. If you die with unconfessed sin, you will still confess this sin, but you will be talking directly to Jesus in paradise. But you are still saved. We are saved by faith in Jesus not by confessing.

I just became a Christian. Do I need to spend 10 hours confessing every sin I have ever committed?

Good Question. All of us have things about which we feel guilty in our past. They can drudge up intense feelings of shame and guilt when we remember them. Our confession of those things puts a stake in the ground. The enemy, Satan, spends his time accusing us over and over about failures from our past. He wants us to live in guilt. God wants us to be free from guilt and shame. This is where confession brings freedom and stops the guilt cycle. Some Christians make a point to spend an extended time confessing every sin they can remember. Most just wait for the Holy Spirit to bring up sins as they live life, both from their past or present, and confess them at that time. There is no specific guide on this from the Bible. God will show you. Give yourself time and be gracious to yourself. Your path to feeling as forgiven as you really are may take time.

Do I ever need to confess to other people?

Yes, for several reasons. First, when your sin affects another person in a direct way, it would be appropriate to confess to them after confessing to God. If you are married, confessing to your spouse when you treat him or her wrongly is an indispensable key to maintaining a healthy relationship. Second, confession to a trusted friend or group of friends is powerful, even if they haven't suffered consequences of your errors. James 5:16 says, *"Confess your sins to each other and pray for each other so that you may be healed."* Sometimes the cycle of a particularly difficult type of addictive entrenched sin can be broken by confessing to friends. It brings healing. This might be a process that takes time. Only confess to friends whose maturity you trust and who understand the grace of Jesus.

So that is it? All I have to do is confess when I sin?

No. That is not it. Tomorrow we will look at what else we do after we confess.

DAY 16
I did it again, part 2 (repentance)

When we sin as followers of Jesus, our first step is to simply agree with God. We do the exact opposite of what Adam and Eve did. We don't hide. We don't blame others, and we don't live in shame. We don't accept negative labels from Satan. Instead, we confidently approach God (Hebrews 4:16) and we own our sin. We tell God what we did, and we accept and acknowledge our forgiveness. But it doesn't stop there. In order to change, we also have to put some flesh into the deal. This involves repentance. When we sin, at some level, we have accepted a false view of God, life, or ourselves. Our mind is thinking incorrectly. In order to break a cycle, we need to repent, which means that we change our minds about what we did and start on a new path.

Read Acts 26:20. This is Paul explaining his teaching.

> I declared to those in Damascus first, and
> then to those in Jerusalem and in all
> Judea, and to the Gentiles, that they should
> repent and turn to God, performing deeds
> consistent with repentance

Definition of *repentance*: A change of mind. Taking a U-Turn. Rethinking life in light of what God says.

In what way did your salvation involve repentance, changing your mind about something?

Look back on the day you were saved. What changes have you made since then?

Read Matthew 3:8 (NIV) (John the Baptist is speaking):

Produce fruit in keeping with repentance.

What "fruit" should accompany our repentance from a sin? Give an example.

Isn't it enough to simply change our minds but not change our lives? Why or why not?

Read Ephesians 4:25-29 (NLT):

So stop telling lies. Let us tell our neighbors the truth, for we are all parts of the same body. And don't sin by letting anger control you. Don't let the sun go down while you are still angry, for anger gives a foothold to the devil. If you are a thief, quit stealing. Instead, use your hands for good hard work, and then give generously to others in need. Don't use foul or abusive language. Let everything you say be good and helpful, so that your words will be an encouragement to those who hear them.

What examples do you see of repentance from specific sins in this passage?

Think of a sin you have committed recently. What changes in your life should accompany your repentance?

WRAP UP

When we, as followers of Jesus, realize that we have sinned, we handle it by doing the opposite of Adam and Eve. First, we confess it, and then we repent. Repentance means that we change our mind about what we did wrong, and we line it up with God's way of living. When John the Baptist says, *"Produce fruit in keeping with repentance,"* he is saying that when we change our mind about our sin, it leads to changed behavior. A changed mind leads to a changed life. Notice that in Ephesians 4:25-29 that you read above, the changed actions that Paul lists are both negative and positive. Stop doing something bad and replace it with something healthy. For example: *"If you are a thief, quit stealing. Instead, use your hands for good hard work, and then give generously to others in need."* Sometimes we struggle to change our behavior even after we have repented. Often this is because we only go halfway. We try to stop doing something without replacing it with a healthy alternative. Often this is frustrating and ends in failure because our sin is usually an unhealthy way of seeking a healthy desire. We need to study the desire that led to our sin and find a healthy way to address that desire. Sometimes our sin comes from trauma that happened in our life, often when we were young. Part of repenting of these types of sins will involve bringing healing from this trauma and letting God's light shine on the painful things that have happened to us. This will loosen the grip that a particular sin has on us.

The practice of repentance is not something you will do a few times and then move on. You will be confessing and repenting for the rest of your Christian life. It is part of a healthy growing relationship with Jesus. Your salvation started with an act of repentance. With God's help, you changed your mind about God. But you will notice that, as you start walking with him, little by little, the Holy Spirit will start pointing out things in your life that he wants you to change – how you treat people, how you use your money, your sex life, your selfishness. Although God saved us exactly as we are, he loves us too much to keep us where we are. He invites us into a better way to live.

It needs to be said that sometimes repentance is hard. Really hard. Changing attitudes and behaviors that have been deeply rooted in our lives for years, possibly since childhood, is seldom a quick and easy process. It is hard work. It involves failure. We cannot do it alone. We need other trusted people to help us in the trenches, especially other Christians who are further down the road than we. This is hard work, but it is worth the effort.

Every Christian, from the person who started walking with Jesus yesterday to the person who has been walking with Jesus for 50 years, will need to walk through these steps for the rest of their lives. This is how we grow. This is basic training.

NEXT LESSON

Let's look at another component of growth: spiritual nourishment.

DAY 17
Spiritual Food

It may sound obvious, but no one grows without eating. If you go a certain amount of time without food, your body starts to fall apart. This is true spiritually as well. In order for us to grow in our faith, we need to eat spiritual food. We need it regularly, or we will not grow. Today we will look at how the Bible provides our soul with spiritual nutrition and how to use it so that we grow.

In Matthew 4 Jesus goes into the wilderness to fast, and he becomes hungry. Then Satan comes to tempt him, trying to repeat what he had done in the garden with Adam and Eve. Read Matthew 4:3-4 (NLT):

> *During that time the devil came and said to him, "If you are the Son of God, tell these stones to become loaves of bread." But Jesus told him, "No! The Scriptures say, 'People do not live by bread alone, but by every word that comes from the mouth of God.'"*

What was wrong with what Satan was suggesting? What was wrong with Jesus turning stones into bread?

In what way is God's word like food for us?

Read 2 Timothy 3:16-17 (NLT):

> *All Scripture is inspired by God and is useful to teach us what is true and to make us realize what is wrong in our lives. It corrects us when we are wrong and teaches us to do what is right. God uses it to prepare and equip his people to do every good work.*

When we look at the benefits of God's word, why is it important that it's inspired by God?

From 2 Timothy 3:16-17, list the different purposes that God's word accomplishes in our lives.

Read Hebrews 4:12 (NIV):

> *For the word of God is alive and active. Sharper than any double-edged sword, it penetrates even to dividing soul and spirit, joints and marrow; it judges the thoughts and attitudes of the heart.*

How does the Bible judge the "thoughts and attitudes of the heart?"

Why do our thoughts and attitudes need to be judged?

WRAP UP

When Satan tempts Jesus to turn stones into bread, he is addressing a valid desire. Jesus was hungry. It eerily parallels what happened in the garden with Adam and Eve. However, Jesus does not fall for the deception. His response is that he hungers for God's word more than bread. He lets his hunger go unsatisfied in order to face down Satan. He is saying to Satan, "*I don't care what physical hunger I have, God's word is my food. It governs all of my other desires.*" This deflates Satan's deception. When Jesus says that we live on every word that comes out of the mouth of God, he is drawing a parallel. God's word is food for our souls. We need to eat it every day, or we become weak. Colossians 3:16 (ESV) says, "*Let the word of Christ dwell in you richly. . .*" This is one habit that is fruitful for you to develop in your life. God wants every person who bumps into Jesus to start nourishing their soul with his word. Make this a daily habit, like eating breakfast. The good news is that you are already doing this! For the last

17 days you have been nourishing your soul. Each lesson you complete, each scripture you read is making you stronger and your soul better nourished. God's desire is for this habit to continue long after you finish *Basic Training*. If you want to grow as a follower of Jesus, this is something you will do for the rest of your life.

The word *Bible* in Greek means book or scroll. Christians first started referring to the Scriptures as "the Bible" in the 2nd century AD, but they used the plural form of the word: The Books. This makes sense because the Bible is a collection of 66 books. There are two major sections. The Old Testament has 39 books that cover the creation of the world through the story of Israel. In it we have history, poetry, wisdom, prophecy and even sex. Jewish boys were not allowed to read Song of Solomon until they were 12 years old because of the sexual content. The New Testament has 27 books and focuses on Jesus. The first four books, called The Gospels, are the story of Jesus, his life, and teachings. The next book, Acts (or Acts of the Apostles), shows us how the church got started and spread throughout the world. The rest of the books are letters to churches in the 1st century AD instructing them how to grow in their faith. The New Testament ends with a book called Revelation (or the Apocalypse) which is a prophetic description of the end of the world and Jesus' return to earth to reign as King.

We can trust that the Bible will feed us because it is inspired by God. It is "God breathed." It has authority in our lives. However, the Bible doesn't do us any good unless we put ourselves under its authority. We grow when we adjust our lives to God's teaching. According to 2 Timothy 3:16-17, the Bible teaches us God's truth about our lives. It shows us where we don't line up with that truth. It then corrects our behavior by teaching us a better way to live and think. And it trains us to live fruitful lives for God in this world. When we put ourselves under the authority of the Bible, our lives start to line up more and more with the better life that God offers us. Our character looks more and more like the character of Jesus.

This all sounds nice, but in reality, it can be quite painful. God's word can hurt. It shines light on areas of our lives that we prefer to keep in the dark. It asks us to make difficult changes. It even convicts us of subtle errors: attitudes, thoughts, and motives. It cuts deep. So this needs to be sold with honesty. Committing to filling your mind with God's word on a daily basis will result in some painful discoveries. But that is where growth starts. You cannot go through basic training without suffering. In the end, if you do not give up, God will use his word to change your life in ways you never thought possible.

NEXT LESSON

How do we communicate with God?

DAY 18

Prayer: Our conversation with God

Communication is an essential factor in a healthy relationship. It is impossible to have a growing friendship with someone without communication. This includes our relationship with God. Today we are going to look at prayer, our conversation with God. Why should we talk with God? What do we talk about? Are there things that I should not bring up to God? What if I don't know what to say?

Read Philippians 4:6-7 (NIV):

> *Do not be anxious about anything, but in every situation, by prayer and petition, with thanksgiving, present your requests to God. And the peace of God, which transcends all understanding, will guard your hearts and your minds in Christ Jesus.*

What things in life make you anxious? How do you normally handle your anxiety?

Why should we pray "with thanksgiving?"

According to this scripture, in what situations should we NOT pray?

What does this passage promise if we pray through our anxiety?

Read what Jesus teaches on prayer in Matthew 6:5-13 (NLT):

> *When you pray, don't be like the hypocrites who love to pray publicly on street corners and in the synagogues where everyone can see them. I tell you the truth, that is all the reward they will ever get. But when you pray, go away by yourself, shut the door behind you, and pray to your Father in private. Then your Father, who sees everything, will reward you. When you pray, don't babble on and on as people of other religions do. They think their prayers are answered merely by repeating their words again and again. Don't be like them, for your Father knows exactly what you need even before you ask him! Pray like this:*

Our Father in heaven, may your name be kept holy. May your Kingdom come soon. May your will be done on earth, as it is in heaven. Give us today the food we need, and forgive us our sins, as we have forgiven those who sin against us. And don't let us yield to temptation, but rescue us from the evil one.

What are some DOs and DON'Ts of prayer?

If God knows what we need before we ask him, why pray?

Read 1 Thessalonians 5:17-18 (NLT):

Never stop praying. Be thankful in all circumstances, for this is God's will for you who belong to Christ Jesus.

How often should we pray?

Doesn't God get tired of hearing us pray?

WRAP UP

Prayer is simply talking with God. It is not a mistake that prayer is often mentioned in the context of anxiety. 1 Peter 5:7 (NIV) says, *"Cast all your anxiety on him because he cares for you."* Prayer is meant to be refreshing to our soul in a world filled with worry. Notice that Philippians 4 does not say that we will get whatever we ask for when we pray. God will answer our requests in one of three ways: yes, no, or wait. But each time we pray we receive a peace and connection with God that is beyond explanation.

There are only two DON'Ts of prayer in Jesus' teaching. First, don't pray so that people see you and are impressed. This type of prayer isn't really prayer; it is acting. Second, don't pray by repeating the same thing over and over, supposing that God will hear you because of the quantity of your words. Remember that this is a relationship. God is not a vending machine or a genie in a bottle. There are no magic words to get what you want. He is your Father who loves you. Talk to him like you are a child talking to your loving father.

Other than that, the sky is the limit. God gives us freedom in how we want to talk with him. We don't have to be in a church or kneel down. We don't have to speak with an

English accent and use "thee" and "thine." Just talk with him, praise him, thank him, make requests, cry, laugh and be who you are. Thanksgiving is an important way to enter into prayer. When we start praying by thanking God for his love and for good things he has done, it puts everything else in perspective. Thanksgiving helps us sense God's presence, and this brings us peace.

In difficult times the Bible says, *"Pour out your hearts to him, for God is our refuge"* (Psalm 62:8, NLT). Prayer deepens our intimacy with God. Prayer can involve fasting, going out in nature, being alone and being with others. Jesus frequently withdrew to the wilderness to pray alone (Luke 5:16). In the hours before he was arrested and killed, he poured his heart out to God in agony (Matthew 26:36-46).

There is a saying among Christians in China: "Little prayer, little power. Much prayer, much power." If you read through the first four books of the New Testament (Matthew, Mark, Luke, and John) and mark every time that Jesus prays, you will realize that he lived a life saturated in prayer. That is Jesus' goal for you too. Prayer is not just making requests. It is a way we enjoy God's presence at all times, and it expresses our dependence on him. Prayer is an essential element in your growth as a follower of Jesus. It is part of your basic training.

NEXT LESSON

What else to do we need in order to grow?

DAY 19
Life in community

What does a life completely dedicated to seeking and walking with Jesus look like to you? Often, we think of a life of solitude, living on top of a mountain and growing a long grey beard. People make long treks to seek words of wisdom from you. Is that what spiritual depth looks like? Is that what God wants? The picture that is painted in the Bible is different, so let's take a look.

Read Acts 2:42-47 (NIV) about how the first Christians lived:

> *They devoted themselves to the apostles' teaching and to fellowship, to the breaking of bread and to prayer. Everyone was filled with awe at the many wonders and signs performed by the apostles. All the believers were together and had everything in common. They sold property and possessions to give to anyone who had need. Every day they continued to meet together in the temple courts. They broke bread in their homes and ate together with glad and sincere hearts, praising God and enjoying the favor of all the people. And the Lord added to their number daily those who were being saved.*

If you look at what the church devoted itself to in Acts 2:42, how does your life line up with this example?

What strikes you about the way they lived out their faith?

Have you ever lived like this before, in intentional community? What keeps you from living this way?

Why might eating together be important?

Read Proverbs 27:17 (NLT):

> As iron sharpens iron, so one person
> sharpens another.

How do we sharpen ourselves as followers of Jesus?

What does it look like for one person to sharpen another?

Read the following verses.

> But encourage one another daily, as long as it is
> called "Today," so that none of you may be
> hardened by sin's deceitfulness (Hebrews 3:13,
> NIV).

> And let us consider how to stir up one another to
> love and good works, not neglecting to meet
> together, as is the habit of some, but encouraging
> one another, and all the more as you see the Day
> drawing near (Hebrews 10:24-25, ESV).

Why might it be unhealthy to live our Christian lives in isolation?

What are the benefits of living in connection with other followers of Jesus?

Why might we have the habit of neglecting to regularly gather with other believers?

Why do we need encouragement?

WRAP UP

The life of spiritual depth and growth is a shared life. We need each other to keep us sharp, for encouragement, and to protect us from being hardened by the deceitfulness of sin. We are much more vulnerable to being tricked or deceived by Satan when we are alone. If you observe the life of the church in the first century, they pursued a life of intentional community. They supported each other financially in hard times. They ate together. There is something powerful about sharing a meal with others. It fosters conversation and connection that doesn't occur in other contexts. They also studied the Bible and prayed together. We have a hard time with this as Americans. We value our privacy and feel like we need to spend hours cleaning our home in order to invite someone over for dinner. We are also really busy. This may be an area of life where we, as followers of Jesus, should live counter-culturally, but it involves sacrifice and a change of priorities.

You might ask, "Should I study the Bible and pray alone or with other people?" And the answer is, "Yes." A healthy mix of personal private devotion and seeking God with others fosters balanced growth. We see both in Jesus' life. But, as followers of Jesus, we cannot do it alone. We need encouragement because life is hard. Galatians 6:2 (ESV) says, *"Bear one another's burdens, and so fulfill the law of Christ."* The Army has a saying: "I will never leave a fallen comrade." We need to be connected to other people who are going in the same direction in order to survive. We become dull on our own, and we need others to sharpen us. This involves opening ourselves up to others and sharing our struggles. We share both victories and failures, because God uses both to teach us and sharpen us. But often we need insight from other more mature Christians to give us perspective. We also need to be challenged in our faith. On our own it is easy to settle down, get comfortable and stop growing.

So the question is this: where do you need to make some changes in your life to make this happen? Maybe you can dedicate a lunch hour each week or an early morning to meet with others and study the Bible. Maybe you need to take a step and attend a Men's or Women's Retreat. Maybe you need to get involved in a home group to study the Bible and pray with people from your community. You need to make an effort to connect with people in a smaller context. Take advantage of all that your church offers to help you grow with other people. Or start a group yourself and invite friends and families to start meeting and seeking God together.

NEXT LESSON

Why does God keep us here on earth? What are we supposed to accomplish?

DAY 20
Come and see - Spreading the news

What purpose does God have for us once we are saved? What does God want us to do with our time and effort here on earth? Are we supposed to wait around until we die so that we can be in heaven with God? Or is there work to do here for God's kingdom? This is what we will look at today.

Read an important task Jesus gives us in Matthew 28:18-20 (NLT):

> Jesus came and told his disciples, "I have been given all authority in heaven and on earth. Therefore, go and make disciples of all the nations, baptizing them in the name of the Father and the Son and the Holy Spirit. Teach these new disciples to obey all the commands I have given you. And be sure of this: I am with you always, even to the end of the age."

Why does Jesus start this command by telling us that he has authority over everything?

How does one go about "making disciples?"

In addition to telling people the good news about Jesus, what else are we supposed to tell them?

Will Jesus leave us alone to accomplish this task?

Re-read Act 1:8 (NLT) that we read several days ago (Jesus is speaking):

> But you will receive power when the Holy Spirit comes upon you. And you will be my witnesses, telling people about me everywhere—in Jerusalem, throughout Judea, in Samaria, and to the ends of the earth.

Why do we need power in order to tell people about Jesus?

What if I don't feel qualified to do this?

Read 1 Peter 3:15 (ESV):

> . . .but in your hearts honor Christ the Lord as holy,
> always being prepared to make a defense to anyone
> who asks you for a reason for the hope that is in you;
> yet do it with gentleness and respect.

When someone asks us about our hope in Jesus, how should we respond?

WRAP UP

Why doesn't God magically transport us off of planet earth when we are saved? If our eternal destiny is with him, why keep us here? The answer is probably not what you have heard: God didn't save us just for heaven. He saved us for earth. He wants to use his church to literally change the world. Jesus entrusted his message of life to his 12 friends before he left earth and ascended to the Father. Think about that. Twelve men. Young men at that. They were all probably in their teens and early twenties. Would you entrust the only plan for saving the human race to them, a bunch of teenagers?

The same goes for us. If you look around, you quickly realize that we are all pretty messed up. And yet God has given this task to us, his followers. We are responsible for two things. First to make disciples. We are charged with the task of telling people who don't know Jesus about his amazing love and grace. What if you don't feel qualified to do this? What if they ask a question you can't answer? It is important to remember that we simply need to tell people about Jesus. Tell them your story. Invite them to church and tell them to read one of the first four books of the New Testament. That isn't so hard is it? All you are really saying is, "Come and see." The one qualifier that we are given is to do this "with gentleness and respect." We should NEVER be pushy or obnoxious. If someone doesn't want to hear about Jesus, you don't need to tell them. Love them and treat them with respect. We don't convert or change anyone. That is the Holy Spirit's job. Jesus has the authority and the Holy Spirit has the power to change lives. We just need to be willing to tell them.

The second thing we are responsible for is to teach new Christians how to obey everything that Jesus has taught us. The word *disciple* means student. In other words, help them grow in their faith by coming under Jesus as his student. When someone around us bumps into Jesus and is saved, we don't leave them where they are. We help them grow. A good place to start would be to take them through *Basic Training*. Give them this book and tell them to start working through it. Then meet with them weekly and discuss what they are learning. You don't have to be a Bible scholar to do this. Jesus entrusted this task to uneducated teenage fishermen. We should be able to do it too.

When Jesus tells his disciples to be witnesses for him in *"Jerusalem, throughout Judea, in Samaria, and to the ends of the earth,"* the equivalent for us would be, "in your city, your state, throughout the entire country, and to the ends of the earth." In other words, we spread the news of Jesus everywhere, both near and far. Do this in your family and neighborhood and go on a trip to far off places like Afghanistan, Uganda, South Sudan, or Mexico City. Jesus' rescue plan is for planet earth, not just a certain country. God wants the good news of his love and forgiveness to spread around the world, and he wants you to be a part of this work. Wherever God takes you in life, he wants you to tell people about Jesus and then teach them how to obey everything that Jesus taught. This is the primary purpose of Jesus' church on earth.

There is much more to learn about being a disciple of Jesus than can be included in this book. This will be an area of learning and growth for you for the rest of your life. The one prerequisite for you to be able to make disciples is that you are a disciple of Jesus yourself! This means that you are working on your own life first to align your inner character and outer behavior to what we see in the life of Jesus. Being a disciple of Jesus is hard. We often fail. When Jesus teaches about the how to be his disciple, he always comments on how difficult it is. Prepare yourself for the journey. It is arduous, but it is an exciting adventure. Remember that Jesus promises to walk with you every step of the way.

NEXT LESSON

There is more to our work on earth than telling people about Jesus.

DAY 21

Service – Bringing God's Kingdom to the World

Is there anything else I'm supposed to do? I understand that I need to tell people about the awesome love and grace of God revealed to us in Jesus, and I need to help them grow in their faith and become disciples of Jesus. Is there anything else? The answer is a big YES. Not only are we to spread the great news about salvation in Jesus, but we need to pull up our sleeves and get our hands dirty. Doing what? That is what we will study today.

Read John 2:13-17 (ESV):

> The Passover of the Jews was at hand, and Jesus went up to Jerusalem. In the temple he found those who were selling oxen and sheep and pigeons, and the money-changers sitting there. And making a whip of cords, he drove them all out of the temple, with the sheep and oxen. And he poured out the coins of the money-changers and overturned their tables. And he told those who sold the pigeons, "Take these things away; do not make my Father's house a house of trade." His disciples remembered that it was written, "Zeal for your house will consume me."

Does Jesus making a whip, turning over tables, and pouring out coins seem like "good Christian behavior?" Why or why not?

What do you think motivated him to take such drastic action?

Read James 1:27 (NLT):

> *Pure and genuine religion in the sight of God the Father means caring for orphans and widows in their distress and refusing to let the world corrupt you.*

Is James' definition of religion what you think of when you hear the word *religion*?

Why would God single out orphans and widows for special care?

Read Proverbs 14:31 (ESV):

Whoever oppresses the poor shows contempt for their Maker, but whoever is kind to the needy honors God.

How is our treatment of the poor tied to what we believe about God?

WRAP UP

Jesus' half-brother, James, defines true religion as *"caring for orphans and widows in their distress and refusing to let the world corrupt you."* This agrees with what Jesus did when he drove out vendors from the temple. It angered him because the sellers put a financial barrier between people and God, and this practice disproportionately impacted the poor. When rich people came to the temple, they brought animals from their own personal farms. The poor however did not and had to purchase their animals for sacrifice. The fact that pigeons are mentioned is significant. Pigeons are what the poorest people sacrificed since they could not afford an ox or sheep. And the venders would sell the animals at prices much higher than market price since they had a captive audience. Jesus got angry. He stewed as he made a whip from scratch, and then he expressed his anger in a healthy way. We often think of anger as being a negative trait, but it can be powerfully good when expressed in the protection of the oppressed.

So we, as followers of Jesus, not only share the good news of forgiveness in Jesus. We also go into society and protect and serve the most vulnerable: widows, orphans, the poor, the sick, single parents, immigrants, and people with disabilities. And sometimes it gets dangerous. When we expose power structures that particularly harm the most vulnerable, we can find ourselves experiencing harsh opposition. However, it is a part of lining our lives up with Jesus. In God's economy the most vulnerable people in society carry an extra weight of importance. As we read in Proverbs 14, God takes note of how we treat the poor, the most vulnerable people in our world. They are the easiest to take advantage of because they don't have resources to fight back. Part of the restoration of shalom on earth is stopping slavery, eliminating discrimination, ending child abductions for prostitution, stopping corruption, and helping widows and orphans. We are slowly, step by step, working to bring shalom back to planet earth.

It can seem overwhelming to know where to get involved in helping. There are so many needs both inside and outside the walls of your church. Ask your pastor to share opportunities to serve locally and internationally. There also might be opportunities in your own neighborhood or community. You don't need to wait around for someone else to lead. Go for it! That is how many of the causes that churches support got started. Someone saw a need and did something. Then it snowballed. It is time for you to get involved in restoring shalom. Who knows? Ask God where he would like to use you to bring shalom to your community. Maybe he will call you to serve on the frontlines protecting people in need. In doing that, you line up your heart with the heart of God.

DAY 22
Growth Plan

Today is the last day of *Basic Training for Walking with Jesus*. You have just dedicated 21 days of your life to study God's word and see how to start building your life on a foundation of solid rock. That rock is Jesus and his teaching. You have studied our salvation. We looked at God, his character, and his nature. We studied about the interesting and mysterious relationship between the Father, the Son, and the Holy Spirit. We also studied how we grow after being saved so that we become mature. This last lesson is a plan for your growth. A popular saying goes, "If you fail to plan, you plan to fail." You have just received good information, life changing information. But it will do you no good if you do not make a plan and put some flesh into it. At the same time, my plan may not work for you, so the goal is not that you adopt a specific plan. The intention is that you make goals that work for you. Your plan does not need to be complicated. It is better to have a plan that is realistic and attainable. At the same time, don't let it become a burden that you dread. The ultimate goal for this plan is to provide intentionality in spending time with your Father, who loves you. As you soak up his word and let it saturate your mind, the Holy Spirit will cause you to grow, to become stronger in your faith. As you pour your heart out to God, his presence will begin to occupy all areas of your thought life. This, in turn, will prepare you to serve him in this world.

Under each category below, write what you want to do, how often, and how long (if applicable). Some of these categories will be daily activities and others will be something you do once a year or every other year. Some may be hard to plan. It is OK to leave one blank.

I have included a plan outline to give you an idea. There are five areas of growth where you can think, pray, and make a plan. It doesn't have to be perfect, and some categories can be left blank for now until you have some clarity. It can always be adjusted if it isn't working. If you are a new believer, reading through the entire New Testament would be a good place to start. Your church can help you with that. It may take you more than a year to complete, but it is a good first step. As you grow and become more mature in Christ, you will add other practices that aren't mentioned in *Basic Training*. God will guide you in this, and he will often use the Christians around you. These five categories are first steps on your path to maturity in Christ.

You are starting out on an exciting adventure!

Here are the five categories with some possible suggestions

BIBLE

> A common habit is to read some of the New Testament each day. If you are a new Christian, this is the perfect place to start. A common plan is to read one chapter from the narrative books of the New Testament (Matthew, Mark, Luke, John,

and Acts) and one chapter from the teaching books (Romans to Revelation) each day. I've done this for many years. After a few years you might want to work in some of the Old Testament too. Ask for recommendations from a Christian who is further down the road than you.

As you read God's word, think about what it reveals about him and you. Is God encouraging you? Is he exposing lies that you believe? Is he urging you to do something? If I sense that God's word is impressing something on me, I will write it down so that I don't forget it. I have gone back and read what I have learned over the years. It is enlightening to see all the ways God has spoken to me through his word.

Think about what time of the day would work best for you. Many people prefer the morning since you start your day orienting your mind towards God. Others are not morning people, so a lunch time or evening works better. Don't read so much that you get saturated. You want to be able to think and meditate about what you read during the day.

PRAYER

You want to have a time to pray every day. It is OK to have some prayer that is organized and scheduled. For example, I pray for a different family member each day of the week. In addition, you want unscripted time to talk with God and enjoy his presence. The Holy Spirit will guide you. An extended time of silence, just being quiet before God, also helps to slow us down and quiet our souls. You also want to develop the habit of praying throughout the day, as a way of living interactively with God.

COMMUNITY

What changes in your life can you make in order to live in intentional community? This can be as simple as opening up your home and inviting people for a meal. It can mean joining a Bible study or going to a men's or women's retreat. There are many opportunities, both inside and outside the church, and you need to be sensitive to work and family. But, as a follower of Jesus, you benefit from living in community with other believers. You grow more as a Christian and live a more balanced spiritual life.

SHARE

What steps can you take to bring Jesus' grace and truth to your family, neighborhood, friends, and work? Do you seek to love and serve your neighbors and stop and talk when they are outside? Are you praying for the people in your neighborhood and work? Whatever you do, don't be weird or force the conversation to be about Jesus. Just love people. Serve them and treat them like Jesus treated people. Who knows? Someday the door might open for you to talk to them about Jesus or invite them to church. Even if that never happens, we are still called to love and serve people.

SERVICE

Start this category with prayer. Ask God to show you where he wants you to serve other people, especially the most vulnerable. Ask him to give you desires. He will hear you and direct your path. For ideas, go to one of your pastors or leaders and ask where the church is involved, both here locally and internationally. This may seem like small things. Taking a meal to your elderly neighbor. Offering to watch a young couple's children so that they can go out together to have a meal. When we love the people around us with Christ's love in seemingly small ways, God uses us in ways that are bigger than we can imagine.

Now go to the next page and prayerfully make a plan.

SPIRITUAL GROWTH PLAN

But grow in the grace and knowledge of our Lord and Savior Jesus Christ. To him be the glory both now and to the day of eternity. Amen (2 Peter 3:18, ESV).

BIBLE

PRAYER

COMMUNITY

SHARE

SERVICE

About the Author

Michel Hendricks has been a pastor, missionary, inventor and author. He has been teaching and training for over 25 years. He is a former pastor of spiritual formation at Flatirons Community Church in Lafayette, Colorado. In addition, he served and trained people in Argentina, Mexico, Kenya, South Sudan and Uganda.

Michel earned a bachelor's degree in Electrical Engineering and Computer Science from the University of Colorado in Boulder. He earned an MDiv degree from Denver Seminary. He is married to Claudia and they have three adult children.

He can be reached at michel.hendricks@gmail.com.

Made in the USA
Monee, IL
13 January 2025